Freedom & Liberty Take Flight

Photography by: Michael Salmon
Story by: Michael Salmon and Daniel Crandall

See more images by Michael Salmon at

Content copyright © 20024 Michael Salmon and Daniel Rg Crandall

All original artwork and story.
No portion of this book may be reproduced, stored in a retrieval system, or transmitted in any form or by any means—electronic, mechanical, photocopy, recording, scanning, or other forms yet to be invented—without the prior written permission of the publisher or author, except for brief quotations in critical reviews or articles. The authors retain full copyright of their original work and have granted permission to Daniel Rg Crandall Publisher and assigned distribution network for usage in this publication and the creation of related marketing materials.

Full Title:
*Freedom & Liberty Take Flight: Two Handsome Young Eagles
Learn Their Purpose— Encouraging Patriots Across this Great Country*

Cover design, interior layout, and composite images by Daniel Crandall, Visualjah — vjah.com

Original publication design copyright © 2024 Daniel RG Crandall Publisher.

All rights Reserved.

PIXEL
GLYPH
PRESS

pixelglyphpress.com
PIXEL GLYPH PRESS
is an imprint of
Daniel RG Crandall Publisher
Nolensville Road, Nolensville, Tennessee, 37135
June 2024
ISBN: 978-1-956579-79-6

Freedom & Liberty Take Flight

Two Handsome Young Eagles Learn Their Purpose—Encouraging Patriots Across this Great Country

One sunny day,
    in a pine tree high in the sky—
Two large Eagle eggs hatched.
Two baby Eagles popped their heads out,
    while Mama Eagle cooed sweet songs.

Daddy Eagle perched nearby,
    proudly watching, protective and strong.
While baby brother Eagle and baby sister Eagle
    snuggled into the warm nest.

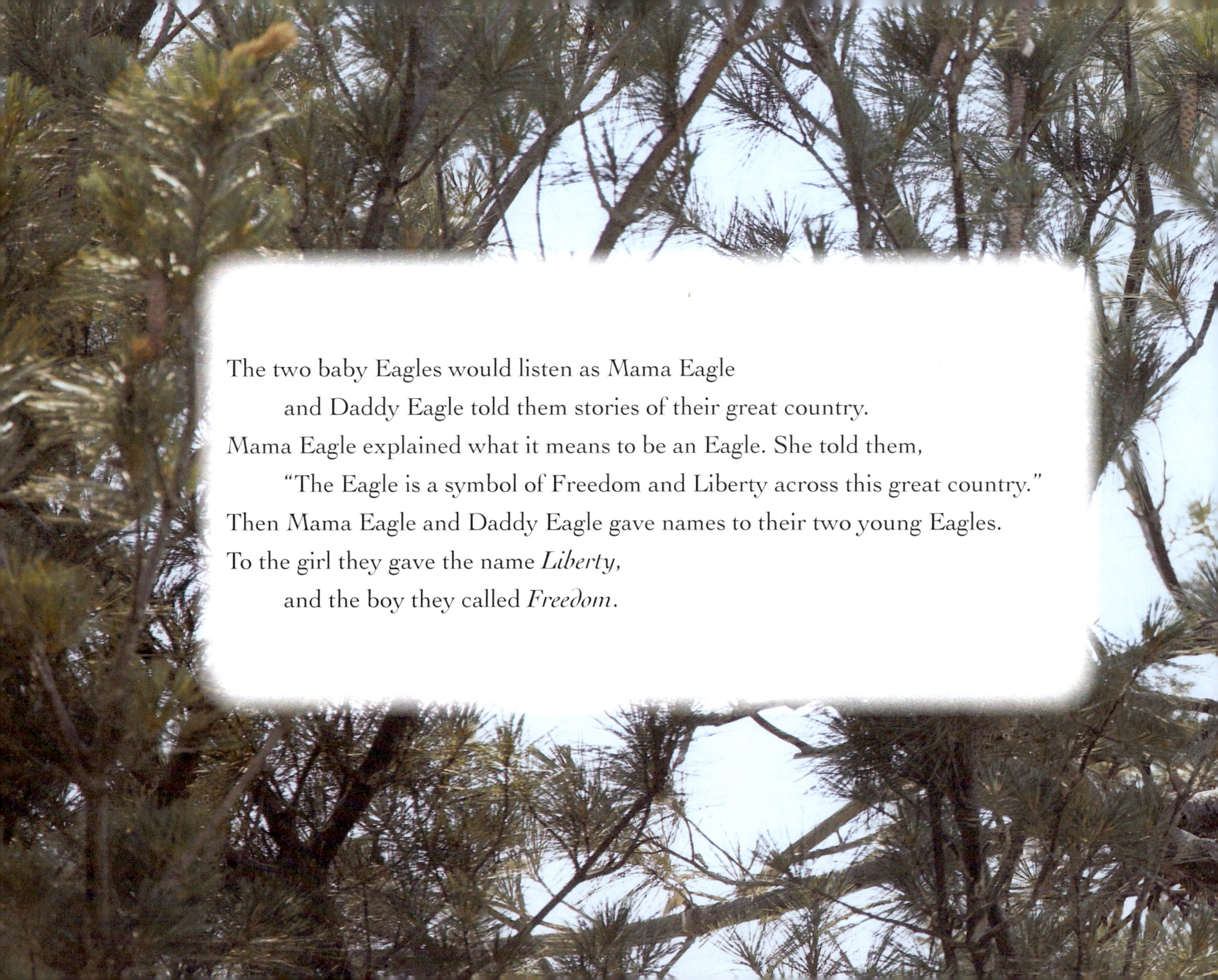

The two baby Eagles would listen as Mama Eagle
 and Daddy Eagle told them stories of their great country.
Mama Eagle explained what it means to be an Eagle. She told them,
 "The Eagle is a symbol of Freedom and Liberty across this great country."
Then Mama Eagle and Daddy Eagle gave names to their two young Eagles.
To the girl they gave the name *Liberty,*
 and the boy they called *Freedom*.

Daddy Eagle would explain the honor and the responsibility of Eagles each day,
    as Liberty and Freedom grew bigger and more powerful.
And every morning as she fed them breakfast, Mama Eagle would remind them
    about the meaning of their names.
Then each night Daddy Eagle would tell them about the important purpose
    and message they would one day carry to the world.

Liberty said to Freedom, "We have a lot to learn. It's a big job"

Freedom said to Liberty, "Together we will stand for Liberty,
    in the land of the brave, and the home of the free."

One morning Daddy Eagle woke them early. "Today is the Day," he said,
    "Today you are leaving the tree.
    You are learning to fly.
    Today, you are free!"

Liberty was scared. They had never left the tree to go down! They didn't know how to fly. And it was a long way to the ground.

"It's okay to be scared," said Mama Eagle, "I know what you can do. You have to hope and trust and be brave. No one can do it for you"

Freedom was very excited, he thought about the meaning of his name. He believed he could do it if he tried.

Freedom jumped up to the edge of the nest. He looked down over the side.

He jumped.

Freedom immediately started to flip through the air, falling, squawking loudly, fighting the wind. It was exhausting and he didn't know what to do. Then he thought he could at least slow down his fall, and he spread his wings to scoop up the air. He found he was able to relax and stop fighting, as his instincts took over.

The Eagle wings of Freedom caught the air and he began to soar.

"I'm flying!" He squawked, but realized the ground was still getting closer and closer. "Eeeek!"

With wings stretched out again he felt them fill with the breeze, then his talons touched the earth.

Flopping to one side, Freedom knew it was not a pretty landing, but he felt safe and strong and proud of his first flight.
He thought to himself, "Today was the first flight of Freedom."

Liberty was next to take the leap.

Her brother watched from the ground as Liberty peaked cautiously over the edge of the nest, high above the top of the pine boughs.

Liberty hesitated, then Daddy Eagle swooped in to give her a little nudge. Liberty went hurling through the sky, tumbling and picking up speed.

"FLY LIBERTY, FLY!" was the call of Freedom.

Falling fast, like Freedom before her, Liberty was ready to give up. Her wings relaxed and spread wide—Immediately, she started to soar!

Nearing the ground, her wings wobbled. Liberty landed with Freedom.

Now Liberty and Freedom would stand together, after surviving their first flight. They overcame the fall, learned to catch the wind, and they were no longer in the nest. The two Eagles were proud of each other, and themselves.

There were many more tumbles and failures, but each passing day they felt their confidence and skills growing.
Liberty would show Freedom how she tightened up her wings and picked up speed.
Freedom would show Liberty how he'd point upward, spin, and flip—talons over beak.

Over the next few weeks, their parents taught Liberty and Freedom how to truly appreciate the beauty and freedom in the wind, how to trust their wings, and to rise above the strongest storms!
They were learning to be the bold Eagles they were made to be.

Liberty and Freedom, both aware they have a greater purpose,
    began to talk about the future.
Freedom dreams of great adventures when he is older, he wants to travel all over
    the United States of America and encourage people to value their freedom.
Liberty loves to dream about growing up into a mature and beautiful Eagle
    with white feathers, and showing people the beauty of liberty for all.

One day Liberty asked, "Daddy? How long until I get white feathers
 like yours and Mama's?"
Her father laughed a loud squawk and said. "You won't get white feathers
 for a few years, but your time will come. You are a beautiful eaglet now.
 Be patient, Liberty! You will one day fly high with white feathers
 and display the beauty of Liberty to this great country."

Liberty and Freedom continued to grow bigger and stronger.

They needed to be fed and defended until Liberty and Freedom had strength to feed and defend themselves.

Their parents were very busy now catching food for them. Both young Eagles agreed—fresh fish from the local river was their favorite.

They continued to practice soaring, eating good food, and growing. Soon they would be strong enough.

"You have both become strong, handsome and beautiful Eagles," Mama Eagle said one day, "Never forget your names—Liberty and Freedom—and what they mean for this country."

"You have made us proud." Daddy Eagle encouraged them both. "Now—Liberty, Freedom—take flight! Soar across this land reminding people to be brave and to stand strong for what is good and what is right—for Freedom and for Liberty."

www.ingramcontent.com/pod-product-compliance
Lightning Source LLC
Chambersburg PA
CBRC100812010526
44107CB00023B/1272